Coach Cal's genius has Enlightened Us to the genius side of Us with his book Favor Rich. *This is what's needed in today's society when people have given up and made to feel inadequate.*

As a mother raising a young woman Favor Rich *is needed to Reinforce the teaching of God's Word, that we're fearfully and wonderfully made, that sounds like God has made us Geniuses. Coach Cal, through* Favor Rich, *has given the tools needed to identify the Genius in you no matter your race, gender, religion or age.*

Favor Rich *inspires you to dream again and that dreams can become a reality. No more dreams dying in the grave but now because of* Favor Rich *your dreams are tangible.*

You can't afford not to read this informative book Favor Rich. *Coach Cal I'm grateful for your Genius to help me Identify that I'm indeed a Genius also!*

– Pastor Kellie White

Whether you are trying to find your purpose, unlock your potential, or optimize your current competencies, Favor Rich *is for you! In this short, but powerful book, Coach Cal explains how everyone is a genius! Moreover, he provides explanations, illustrations, guidelines, and tools that will help you to not only unlock your unique genius, but also to optimize and translate it into action.*

– Dr. Richard D. Harvey
Organizational Effectiveness Consultant and
Professor of Psychology

DISCOVER AND LEVERAGE
YOUR INNER GENIUS AND PURPOSE

FAVOR
RICH

CAL THOMPSON

Favor Rich
Discover and Leverage Your Inner Genius and Purpose
Cal Thompson
Favor Rich Publishing

Published by Favor Rich Publishing, St. Louis, MO
Copyright ©2019 Cal Thompson
All rights reserved.

Editor: Beth Hammock

Interior design: Davis Creative, DavisCreative.com

Library of Congress Cataloging-in-Publication Data
Library of Congress Control Number: 2018914691
Cal Thompson
Favor Rich: Discover and Leverage Your Inner Genius and Purpose
ISBN: 978-1-7335021-0-8 (Paperback)
       978-1-7335021-1-5 (eBook)
       978-1-7335021-3-9 (Case Laminate)
Library of Congress subject headings:

   1. REL012090 RELIGION / Christian Living / Professional Growth

   2. BUS050000 BUSINESS & ECONOMICS / Personal Finance / General

   3. BUS107000 BUSINESS & ECONOMICS / Personal Success

2019

ATTENTION CORPORATIONS, UNIVERSITIES, COLLEGES AND PROFESSIONAL ORGANIZATIONS: Quantity discounts are available on bulk purchases of this book for educational, gift purposes, or as premiums for increasing magazine subscriptions or renewals. Special books or book excerpts can also be created to fit specific needs. For information, please contact Favor Rich Publishing, 224 N. Lindbergh, Ste. 256, Florissant, MO 63031 or Cal@FavorRich.com

DEDICATION & ACKNOWLEDGMENTS

First and foremost, this book is dedicated to my Lord and Savior Jesus Christ. Thank you for sacrificing your life for me. Thank you also for my genius purpose assignment and for giving me the awesome responsibility of introducing *Favor Rich* to the world.

This book is dedicated to my father, William Henry Thompson (1930-2004) and my mother Rosella Thompson. My motivation for trusting God originated with the example I saw displayed in our home. I am a better person because God entrusted me to the two best people I have ever known. I am honored to be called your son!

To my wife, Tellia, of 35 years I dedicate this book to you. May our love grow to reach the boundaries set only by God. Our best times are yet to come! Thanks for the confidence you have shown in me. I am highly favored to be your husband!

To Tiffany, Christian and Symone, my three beautiful jewels, you are geniuses because you are born of God, never forget that. The heights that you can reach are unlimited. I am ecstatic to be your father!

To my three brothers, Frank, Tony, and Terrance and my two sisters, Veronica and Sandra, thanks for believing in me. You all know me best. Your love and commitment to me has encouraged me to excel in life and business. I am blessed to be your brother!

Thanks to the major educators and influencers in my life: Simon T. Bailey, Frank Thompson, Ron Tucker, Dwight McDaniel, Stephen and Kellie White, Dr. Richard Harvey, Jeff Perry, David Blunt, Dr. Bill Winston, T.D. Jakes, David Steward, Joel Osteen, Dr. Raphael Green and Tony Farr.

Thanks to my genius communication consultants: Jack and Cathy Davis, Ellena Balkcom, Sandra Williams, Beth Hammock and Kim Spence. Thanks to Robert Bunch for your animation genius, Frank Thompson, for your musical genius and Edward Carpenter, for your photography genius.

FOREWORD

In life there are times when you access a new revelation that changes the trajectory of your life. Well, *Favor Rich* is the new software of the mind that does it in one swipe and click. Once you download it into your spirit, your life will never be the same again. Coach Cal shows us in a world of automation, algorithms, and artificial intelligence, that genesis of genius lives on the inside of us. As a result of the finished work of Jesus Christ, we're able to accelerate into our destiny using the apps of possibility and potential to create a better world.

Do yourself a favor, read this book twice. Take notes. Teach it to everyone that matters to you. Then buy a copy for someone else. I have already bought copies for my children. I want them to understand the *Favor Rich* revelation and pass it on to my future grandchildren. Thank you, Coach Cal, for hearing a fresh word from the Lord.

I realize that I am Favor Rich and so are YOU!

–Simon T. Bailey, Breakthrough Strategist
and Friend of God

TABLE OF CONTENTS

INTRODUCTION

At the age of 16, I decided that because I was the only one in a family of six without a gift *oozing* out of me, that I'd simply *take* my brother's gift of playing music by ear. My knack for business and entrepreneurship wasn't apparent or glamorous enough for me at that time, and was still somewhat uncovered, so coveting and borrowing someone else's seemed like the logical thing to do in my young mind. Well, when my mother heard the unrecognizable noise coming from my attempts to play the piano, her stern correction quickly told me this was not a bright idea. *Favor Rich* was written to share the good news that you never have to covet, borrow, or mimic anyone else's gift again. In the pages of this book, you'll uncover the preprogrammed attributes that God instilled in you before you were even formed in the womb. As a matter of fact, there's more good news. Everyone, including you, is born with not one, but seven, *divine endowments:* **talents, abilities, gifts, treasure, faith, favor, and purpose**.

Fast forward to present day. One Sunday morning I was invited, by the same brother whose gift I had "borrowed" as a kid, to speak at his church. As he was introducing me, I heard him say on my way to the podium something that made me want to vanish through the floor. He said, "My brother, Cal, is a genius." Instead of feeling flattered or proud, these words were totally embarrassing to me. I had never had anyone at any time refer to me as a genius. I didn't feel worthy and that introduction caught me totally off guard because I did not feel like the genius he was describing.

Several weeks later, while praying in my hotel room in the Washington, D.C. area, I heard the words, "Calvin, you are a genius because my genes are in you." Wow, this blew me away! I had previously felt unworthy to be called a genius. One is not genius based upon their accomplishments. God has favored me to own and operate seven businesses over a thirty-year period. Those businesses have varied in industry and include VIP transportation management, award-winning residential and commercial real estate development, ownership of a conference center with café and coffeehouse, and foreign exchange global trading. However, none of these ventures made me a genius. I have genius inside of me because God is the *genesis* of genius and I am his workmanship. He created me in His image to do good works on earth.

Money does not make you a genius either. I have been entrusted with millions of dollars in business and in real estate. The genius inside of me helped me to manage profitable businesses. This was possible because I had the courage to listen and heed to Godly wisdom. Have I made mistakes? Yes, genius does not mean I am infallible, however, I should always strive to leverage my maximum potential.

That's right, and the same is true for you. Everyone born is an offspring of God, and these seven rich characteristics, or divine endowments, are given despite our behavior and whether we deserve them or not.

I believe that all men are created equal. It's not just a cliché or a constitutional right that we are all equal—it is the reality of how God made us. Everyone who is living and breathing is Favor Rich and filled with special gifts and genius unique to each individual. The amazing thing about Favor is that it is unmerited. That means you can't earn it and don't have to borrow it. It's freely given.

I believe *all* life begins with God, including animals. There are genius abilities and a purpose within all of God's creations. From the ant to the plant; from the bee to the sea; from the tiger to the spider; from the bear to the mare; from the beagle to the eagle, and yes, from the man to the land; all of God's creations have a genius and a purpose within them.

If you've ever studied the complex hierarchal system in which ants work together, you know it's pure genius. The same is true for the complexity of webs that spiders weave and the rituals that fuel the circle of life in the wild. This is genius at its best and every animal has a specific job. It's much easier for one to believe that if ants have genius and purpose within them, then since humans are greater than ants, we too must have a specific genius and purpose within us. It's only when we try to compare ourselves with someone on our level that we feel that we don't measure up. For example, not many people would try to measure their intelligence against Albert Einstein's, because they could easily see his talents, abilities, and gifts oozing out of him. But the real way to know for sure that you have specific genius and purpose is to not to judge yourself by someone that is an equal to you, but to judge yourself by the person who created you and take Him at His Word that He made you in His image and in His likeness.

Furthermore, the genius inside of us is not because of our IQ. Rather, it is because we have our Heavenly Father's DNA. Remember the movie, *Princess Diaries,* when the granddaughter found out she was royalty. That's how I felt after hearing that God's genes were on the inside of me. Royalty is in our blood. Therefore, when you come into the knowledge of whose blood runs through your veins, that in itself, should change your mindset and actions.

God is the genesis of all life. Just as I believe that life begins at conception, I also believe that's when your genius starts. We are God's prized possessions. He is the originator and creator of Genius. As His offspring, we are created in His image and likeness, which means we have His genes and that makes us geniuses.

You need to recognize and appreciate the value and greatness of the human spirit inside you. Look at what and who you were modeled after. Your human spirit was made after the likeness of the Creator of this vast universe. This Creator told the stars to shine in the morning and told the ocean to only come this far and stop. He assigned the galaxies, the sun, and the moon. He commanded each planet in what to grow and what to do.

So, when you wake up in the morning, you can boldly say, "I am a genius, because God's genes are in me!" I have creative power within me because I am made in God's image and likeness. But wait. The promise extends further. You are more than a genius. You are a genius with a purpose, on assignment for our creator. We have been given an assignment, which is buried within us, and we must discover and leverage it to help ourselves and others succeed. This is our divine purpose for being put on this Earth.

Imagine for a moment that you have treasure at the bottom of your soul's core and it needs to be unearthed to see its beauty and worth. If this was an Earthly treasure—gold, diamonds, an inheritance—what lengths would you go to in order to find it and claim it? Then how much more should we do to unveil the richness of our buried gifts meant to be used to build God's Kingdom and fulfill His purpose for our lives?

God, being omniscient, knew us before we were born, and He preplanned our work for us in advance of our birth. He told the prophet Jeremiah, "…before you were formed in your mother's womb, I knew you and ordained you."

God sees the past, present and future, all at the same time. He is aware of all things that concern you. His plans for you are good and He wants you to fulfill His purpose for your life. His plans will bring you to a great expectation that He has prepared especially for you, that can't be duplicated by anyone else. God is rooting for you to discover who you are and what you can do at full potential to make a major impact on this world. In fact, He wants you to dominate in this life, not dominate other people, but your circumstances, and reign in your specific genius and purpose. In *Favor Rich*, you will embark on a journey of self-discovery and uncover how to develop and leverage your inner genius and purpose.

THERE'S AN APP FOR THAT

"...mobile is the digital gateway for the real world to join in this global metamorphosis of human behavior."
– Tomi Ahonen, consultant and speaker

In 2019, we are not only familiar with mobile phones, but our society has become pretty dependent upon them. The quote above is fitting in that these little handheld devices are a portal for all the changes we're seeing in human behavior. Today, if you ever want to learn more about a person, just take a peek at their cell phone and all will be revealed, from what they value to what they spend their money on and what they think about most. Within our mobile phones, we have these little applications (apps) that run programs like Google, Twitter, and Instagram. Each of these has a specific function, and our app downloads are perhaps the most revealing about who we really are. Now that I've uncovered my gift for recognizing needs in the marketplace and inventing solutions, I'd like to think I will come up with the last remaining life-changing app yet to be created. Chances are, though, if you have an interest, hobby or knowledge gap, *there's already an app for that!*

U.S. scientists who measured the storage capacity of the part of the brain that stores memory have discovered that the human brain has a capacity ten times greater than what was first thought and can retain 4.7 billion books. This is roughly one petabyte, or 1,000,000,000,000,000 bytes of information. This means we are all marvelously preprogrammed to be geniuses. Similarly, in our heart drive, God has preprogrammed us with seven rich characteristics, hereafter known as Seven Mobile Apps. These seven apps, including talents, abilities, gifts, treasure, faith, favor, and purpose, are mobile because God knew we would travel from place- to-place and would need 24-7 access to them. When you tap into their potential, they will help you conquer every situation that you will ever face.

Although thousands of apps have been created to help us perform certain tasks, we are not limited by apps already created by others. There are seven apps that are readily available for you to tap into. With these apps, you can supersede any app already in existence. You are able to do this because of your individual genius and God-given purpose. Nobody can fulfill or imitate the unique genius, purpose, creativity, and innovation that lies within YOU.

Each App is uniquely made specifically for you. Your color, gender, height, location, and generation were all factored into your being and assignment, and therefore, nothing can stop you from accomplishing the assignment that God has given you. Nothing that is, except for *you*. Don't shrink back from dreams that you have, because they are hard and may seem impossible. Just remember that every fiber of you was made for this!

Did you know NBA star Michael Jordan was cut during varsity tryouts his sophomore year in high school? Instead, he was forced to play junior varsity. Michael Jordan went on to play 15 seasons as the most revered player in the world and go on to score a career 32,292 points, earn six NBA championships, five NBA MVP titles and make 14 All-Star Game appearances. Every App that was later in him to break these records, was also in him during that varsity tryout. The reason you need to understand the concept of Favor Rich is because you will encounter situations and circumstances in this life that are beyond your control and may even feel hopeless or overwhelming, but in the pages of this book, you will be reminded that inside of you, **"There's an App for That."**

AFFIRMATION STATEMENT

I am not moved by what I see or what I feel. I know that I have greatness within me. I am not a mistake or an after-thought. God was intentional when He created me in His image and in His Likeness. I was created to manifest the glory of God. I am a genius and as my light shines God will get the glory from my life and my very presence will automatically liberate others to display their unique genius!

TAG YOU ARE "IT"

"We all have genius within us,
never doubt that fact."
— Catherine Pulsifer

Most of us played tag as a child, right? In case you didn't, here is the flow of the game. One person is "it." His or her job is to touch someone else. When you are touched by the person who is "it," *you* immediately become "it." Now, it's your job to tag someone else. The game usually continues until everyone decides to stop, or until a predetermined number of people have become "it." This is the only game I know where there was no disappointment in losing. Theoretically, you've lost if you're tagged, but I was equally as excited when I felt the tap of a tag on my shoulder or back, because then I would just tap into the thrill of the chase. That just meant it was time to hurry and tag someone else. I'd call that a win-win.

As a child, I was very good at playing tag because I was elusive, which meant I knew how to hide and make it back to the base (the safe place) without getting tagged, as well as a great ability to move quickly in tagging someone else. Those same attributes followed me in life. As a young man, I was elusive. If someone would ask me my purpose, I would evade answering the question directly by giving a very generic answer. For instance, I would say, "My purpose is to serve God." I just did not know the specific answer because there were no gifts oozing out of me (unlike my siblings).

As an adult, I also had a knack for following through quickly on projects. I knew that I was created to be an entrepreneur, so I was eager to try different startup ventures. This was my attempt to get rich quick or make a boatload of cash. Some of the start-up businesses I have owned are a real estate brokerage, real estate development, limousine company, MLM Travel Company, a conference center with café and coffeehouse, etc. I found myself trying to borrow my way to wealth by getting outside loans to finance my future. I was using information from seminars, under-graduate, and graduate degrees to try to become successful.

While pursuing all these ventures, I remained faithful to God. I attended church to continue to be inspired and motivated. I hid in the church's pews, because I knew that it was a safe place. I also knew the Bible said that God wanted me to prosper and be in health even as my soul prospers. I wanted to avoid being tagged by poverty.

The downside of using world market influences to become significant is that your success depends upon market conditions and the economy. What I failed to understand is that real signifi-cance is an "inside job." I did not understand the riches that had already been deposited in me from birth. I had no idea that inside of me I already had Seven Mobile Apps that made me Favor Rich. I also didn't realize that these apps included specific plans on how to discover and leverage each one of them. I was trying to avoid being tagged with poverty. In reality, I had already been tagged with talents, abilities, gifts, (TAG) treasure, purpose, faith, and favor. I was already significant, plus had genius and real purpose. I was Favor Rich and I didn't even know it! The Seven Mobile Apps that have been deposited in me from birth are backed by Heaven's economy and there are no disruptions there! In fact, the Earth is owned by the same person who put the apps on the inside of me. That means I am backed by the bank of heaven.

Don't try to be elusive to avoid being tagged with poverty. You already have a genius. Inside of you is the power to get wealth. Your job is to discover and leverage your genius, and then go and tag someone else to let them know what they have within them. We are to continue to tag people until everyone realizes that they are "IT" (a genius). Individual unique greatness is already inside each of us.

Many people are searching for the next big idea! They are looking for companies that make it into *Fast Company* magazine's list of successful start-ups! So many people wish they could have gotten on the ground floor of companies like Google, Facebook, Microsoft, Apple, etc.

However, I want you to know that the next big idea is YOU! You are in God's "IT" (genius) department. You are the "Intelligence Tool" (genius) that He will use to make a major impact on this earth. When you discover and leverage your inner genius and purpose, you will have access to unlimited resources to accomplish the reason you were created.

You are God's workmanship, His Masterpiece created for good works which He prepared in advance of creating you. Do you know why you were created? The reason is inside of you! The next big idea is in you and you are the "Intelligent Tool" (genius) that will accomplish the work that God wants to do on Earth.

God is Genius. Everyone has God's DNA (Downloaded Noble Authority) in them; therefore, everyone has genius abilities. The world's view of genius is that it is an inherent feature **among** human beings that distinguishes a few people in the minority (i.e., geniuses) from the majority (i.e., non-geniuses). But my view of genius is that it is an inherent feature **within** every human being. Instead of distinguishing people from one another, it simply distinguishes abilities within people. Thus, each of us has a few genius abilities within us amidst the majority of our non-genius abilities. Say it with me, *God tagged me with Talents, Abilities, and Gifts*.

AFFIRMATION STATEMENT

I carry God's DNA within me, and that makes me a genius. I am equipped and tagged with extraordinary talents, abilities, and gifts, which makes me the next big deal. I'm favored with divine ideas and visions for God's use of my genius abilities and I will use them for His glory.

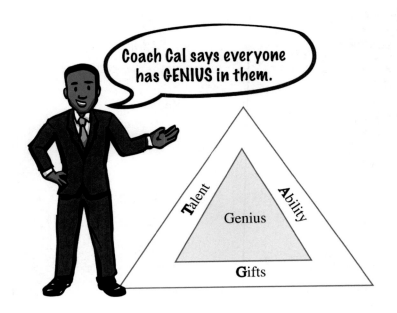

A CLOSER LOOK AT TAG

In the previous chapters, we have discussed the concept of genius. Our genius is revealed through the discovery of our Talents, Abilities, and Gifts our TAGs (See Figure 1). Now, let's further define what TAGs are. Then, we will explore how to properly and divinely assess them. To get you prepared for this chapter, think about these four vital questions:

1. What have you always desired to do?
2. What have you been trained /educated to do?
3. What can you do better than most?
4. What things did you consistently list in numbers one, two, and three?

What you identify in number four is an indicator of your genius. To identify your genius, we will need to take a deeper dive in the TAG concept, definitions, and how to identify them.

Talents

Our talents are generally considered "aptitudes" in that they reflect the potential that is in everyone. These are the natural or raw skills that we are born with. Because they are raw, they tend to be generic with regard to areas of application. That is, they aren't necessarily associated with a specific job or task. For this reason, our talents aren't often visible until they are performed in some capacity. Nevertheless, they can lie undeveloped within us for years or even entire lifetimes without our being aware of them. Here are a few examples of various talent categories.

Table 1: Talent Categories

Categories	Definition
ARTISTIC	Individuals who have this raw talent understand and use artistic principles and methods in different ways. For example, they may draw, decorate, design, create, paint, sculpt, or take photographs.
ATHLETICISM	Individuals with this raw talent have strength, agility, stamina, and/or energy that makes a great athlete. It takes athleticism to run marathons, play pro football, etc.
CLERICAL	Individuals who have this raw talent are very detail-oriented. They prefer to be accurate in their work. Often, they use their eyes, hands, and fingers at the same time to enter figures in books, on forms, and by computer.

INTERPERSONAL	Individuals with this raw talent communicate well with many kinds of people. They are able to be understanding, friendly, and polite in different situations. They like to work with others and contribute to a group with ideas and suggestions.
LANGUAGE	Individuals who have this raw talent like to use spelling, grammar, and punctuation correctly when writing documents such as letters and reports and writing or reporting stories. They desire to speak clearly. They desire to understand and respond to feedback and to ask questions appropriately.
LEADERSHIP/ PERSUASIVE	Individuals who have this raw talent desire influence opinions and actions by presenting their ideas and getting people to work well together to achieve a goal. These individuals have the raw talent to communicate thoughts, feelings, and ideas to support a position.
MANUAL/ TECHNICAL	Individuals who have this raw talent use their hands, fingers, and eyes together to control equipment, to adjust controls on machines, to use hand tools, or to put products together. They can operate and adjust machines/equipment and are able to spot and correct parts that are not functioning.
MUSICAL/ DRAMATIC	Individuals who have this raw talent tend to be musical or dramatic. They may have the raw talent to interpret roles and express ideas and emotions through non-verbal facial gestures and body movements. They might play instruments, sing, or teach or direct music. They may produce, direct, or perform in plays.
NUMERICAL/ MATHEMATICAL	Individuals with numerical and mathematical raw talent like to deal with practical problems in business, technology, or science by choosing correctly from different mathematical techniques. They like to express mathematical ideas in speaking and in writing.
ORGANIZATIONAL	Individuals who have this raw talent know how to decide what is most important so that it is completed first and on-time. They are able to organize, process, and maintain written or computerized records and other forms of information in a way that makes sense.
SCIENTIFIC	Individuals who have this raw talent prefer to apply scientific research findings to problems in medicine, the life sciences, and the natural sciences. They prefer to use logic or scientific thinking to deal with problems or to understand or treat human and animal injuries and illnesses. Often, they base their conclusions on information that can be measured or proved.

SOCIAL	Individuals who have this raw talent use special skills to help others define and solve personal problems. They have the raw talent to deal well with others. Individuals who have this raw talent may gather and study information about others. They may work on a person-to-person basis or with groups.
SPATIAL	Individuals with this raw talent are able to look at objects from one angle and know what they would look like from a different angle. They can look at a rough sketch and understand what the finished product will look like.

Abilities

Abilities are competencies and skills that have been developed. This development has generally taken place across a range of experiences. These experiences may be planned or unplanned. For example, education would be an example of a planned experience. Degrees and certificates of completion are indicators that a person has methodically been exposed to a pre-planned set of educational and/or training experiences. Unplanned experiences entail general hands-on opportunities that have been afforded to us often in a seemingly random way. Regardless of whether the experience has been planned or unplanned (and perhaps a bit of both), it has transformed the raw talent (mere potential) into actual abilities. Unlike talents, abilities are task and job specific. For example, through experience (e.g., education, on-the-job training, etc.) our raw talent for working with numbers was developed into the ability to work with spreadsheets and perhaps do the job of an accountant.

Gifts

Gifts reflect those skills and competencies that we have in which we are able to perform them (i.e., ability) with mastery. In other words, we appear to be a "cut above" others. In a sense, our gifting is often divine in nature. The superior skill with which we are able to perform these tasks/jobs seems to clearly be a matter of grace.

The Genius of TAGS

A key feature of TAGs is the differences in how many we have. We tend to have many more invisible and raw talents than we do abilities and gifts. And likewise, we tend to have more abilities than we have gifts. It is our contention that everyone that God has created has some innate talent (i.e., raw undeveloped potential). Recall the notion that everyone that God created is a genius because they have the genes of God residing within them. Genes are the invisible building blocks of nature (called the genotype). In contrast, the phenotype is the visible manifestation of these invisible genes. However, not all of the genes are manifested in the phenotype. But they are still there. Just because you can't see your talents (i.e., genotype) does not mean that you don't have any. The talents will have to be developed into abilities and gifts to be visible (i.e., the phenotype).

Alignment

The key to unlocking the TAGs app and creating your streams of revenue is in the alignment of the TAGs. That is, there must be consistency between our natural skills (talents), developed skills (abilities), and mastered skills (gifts). Misalignment is what blocks the flow of the stream. Talents that are never developed into abilities simply remain as untapped potential. Abilities that don't flow from natural talents can feel like a drudgery, becoming extremely laborious because of the extra effort that must be put forth when doing something that doesn't come natural to us.

Abilities that don't rise to the level of gifting often reflect minimal qualifications rather than exceptional performance for which one might receive high visibility. Finally, gifts that aren't aligned with abilities constitute exceptional skills that have not been submitted to discipline (associated with the development of abilities). Exceptionally skillful people without discipline occasionally use their gifts to do more harm than good.

The ultimate goal is to identify those skills and competencies for which we have talent, ability, and gifting. If you already have a good handle on what your TAGs are, then great! However, many people do not, and even more people are not aware of all of their potential (talent). Hence, even if you think you have a good feel for yours, you might still benefit by taking a formal assessment that inconclusively leads you to those TAGs that become the foundation of purpose. *

List your Genius from Table 1 Talent Categories to identify those skills and competencies for which you have Talents (natural skills), Abilities (developed skills) and Gifting (mastered skills).

Talents_____

_____

Abilities_____

_____

Gifts_____

_____

AFFIRMATION STATEMENT

I am a genius, because I have God's genes in me. I was created in God's image and in His likeness. Therefore, creativity and witty inventions are a part of my DNA. I have Downloaded Noble Authority (DNA) to dominate the circumstances that I face. The bigger my circumstances are, the harder they will fall. I am already a success because God has ordered my steps. When my Seven Mobile Apps are in alignment with the creator of this vast universe, then the provisions for my ideas are backed by the bank in heaven. My God shall supply all of my needs, according to His riches in Glory, by Christ Jesus.

Notes:

*We recommend *Ability Explorer*, Third Edition (ISBN 978-1-59357-883-1). ©2012 by Joan C. Harrington, Thomas F. Harrington, and Janet E. Wall.

References

Harrington, T., & Harrington, J. (2001). A new generation of self-report methodology and validity evidence of the ability explorer. *Journal of Career Development, 9*, 1, 41–48.

Harrington, T., & Harrington, J. (2002). The ability explorer: Translating Super's ability-related theory propositions into practice. *The Career Development Quarterly, 50,* 4, 350–358.

Harington, J., Harrington, T., & Wall, J. E. (2012). *Ability Explorer*, 3rd Ed. St. Paul, MN: JIST Works. *The Telegraph* (2016). Human Brain Can Store 4.7 billion Books

Hidden Treasure Revealed

I will give you hidden treasures,
riches stored in secret places.
— Isaiah 45:3

Treasure is usually found in two places, either beneath the surface, or hidden in plain sight. Treasure also appears in various forms. It can be visibly beautiful in its natural state, like a pearl, or if you've ever seen untouched gold rocks or nuggets, a treasure can look downright rough and ugly in raw form, until it undergoes a refinement process.

Likewise, the treasure hidden beneath our surface is sometimes not easily identified by the naked eye and in raw form; the beauty of our treasure may not appear brilliant or captivating. Your treasure can also take on many forms and rather than a beautiful talent like my brother's ability to play music by ear, like mine and many others, your treasure could be in your genius in the marketplace and in opportunities that come through the problems you are able to solve and/or the needs you can fulfill. Genius refers to one's God-given and distinctive abilities.

An example of treasure hidden in plain sight, occurred years ago when I was rehabbing real estate properties. I used my God-given entrepreneurial genius to see the value in buildings needing total renovation. I saw the hidden value, which was the real character of a building, although it was ugly from outward appearance and in need of a lot of repair. Others may have viewed that same property as an eyesore that should have been demolished, but I saw the potential of restoration and could envision that same building being brought back to its highest and best use. For my efforts, we received several historical awards and the highest award given by the city for preserving a building in a historical district.

Sometimes it takes tremendous courage to uncover and share the hidden treasures within. This was the case with world renown motivational speaker, Les Brown. As young man, he attempted to deliver his first public speech in front on the entire student body/school. He walked on stage, opened his mouth, but nothing came out. The audience laughed him off the stage. He said he saw the people, and everything that he had planned to say left his mind. If someone saw him and judged him on his first attempt as a speaker, they would have said he did not have any talent or treasure. Now, he is listed as one of the top ten speakers in the country. So, I encourage you not to judge a book by its cover, not even your own. Your treasure needs the discipline of training and sometimes the refinement process of maturity to surface the excellence God intended. The lesson is don't despise small beginnings. You need tests and trials for endurance, to have empathy for others, and to develop your own testimony.

Treasure is also hidden in the cemetery. Consider people who buried the treasure that God gave to them by not using it, so they took it with them to the grave. In Matthew 25:14–30 we learn of a master who was leaving his house to travel and before leaving, entrusted his property to his servants. According to the abilities of each man, one servant received five talents, the second servant received two talents, and the third servant received one talent. The property entrusted to the three servants was worth eight talents. Each *talent* represented a significant amount of money. Upon returning home, after a long absence, the master asked his three servants for an account of the talents he had entrusted to them. The first and the second explained that they each put their talents to work and doubled the value of the property with which they were entrusted; each servant was rewarded. His master said to them, "Well done, good and faithful servants. You have been faithful over a little; I will set you over much. Enter into the joy of your master." — *Matthew 25:23, New English Translation*

The third servant, however, had merely hid his talent, had buried it in the ground, and was punished by his master. *"Therefore, take the talent from him and give it to the one who has ten. For the one who has will be given more, and he will have more than enough. But the one who does not have, even what he has will be taken from him. And throw that worthless slave into the outer darkness, where there will be weeping and gnashing of teeth." — Matthew 25:24–30, New English Translation*

Just because you bury your talent or treasure when you die or decide not to obey what it is that God has given you to do, doesn't mean the talent or treasure will stay buried. The principle here is that God will take from the person who buried their talent (treasure) and he will reassign it to people who are good and faithful. This is God making sure that His word does not come back to Him void.

Sonny knew he was a gifted singer, musician and songwriter, but he never acknowledged, shared his talents, abilities and gifts with anyone.

Treasure hidden in the wisdom of seniors

So, you might ask what happens to your preprogrammed seven apps, including your **talents, abilities, gifts, treasure, faith, favor and purpose, once you become seniors or golden in age?** The answer is clear. As long as there's breath in your body, God *can and will* use willing vessels to advance his agenda on Earth.

The key is for you not to die full of unused or underused talents, abilities and gifts. I encourage you to finish your course and die empty.

In doing a recent search of Forbes' most powerful CEOs, I discovered an article that had me very excited and hopeful about God's plan for seniors. It was about an 87-year-old Chinese CEO and legend, Chu Shijian, who started to build his first empire when he was 51 years old. After 18 years of building, he became known as the king of tobacco in China. At the age of 71, he was put in jail due to some financial problems. Later, at the age of 74, he was allowed to take a conditional release, due to severe diabetes.

Most of us would have thanked God for freedom, and at that age, enjoyed the few years we had left. Not Chu Shijian. He took a few months to get his body in better shape and improve his health, and then began to build his second commercial empire. In 2011, his new company, an orange orchard, earned over 80 million yuan, or $11 million US dollars.

Imagine you are 75 years old and newly released from prison with a feeble body, and your only daughter had committed suicide while you were incarcerated, like Chu's did. What plans would you have made for the rest of your life? I would probably, above all else, want to just *rest*. Chu did just the opposite. He contracted a 2000-acre desolate land in the Ailao Mountains, which he quickly converted to a large orchard planted with thousands of orange trees. He transformed himself and his thinking from the previous tobacco factory boss he had been into a normal working farmer. He spent most of his day in the orchard, trying to find a way to raise both the quality and quantity for each single tree. As a result, Chu built an inspiring system, urged the farmers to get more involved. Each decision he made surprisingly led to successful results.

The article mentions that Wang Shi, who is a great entrepreneur of real-estate in China, once paid a visit to Chu in the mountains, and he was completely overwhelmed by the old man. He said, "It takes six years for an orange tree to begin to yield fruit, and I could never imagine a person doing this at the age of 75." He asked Chu Shijian, "What is your wish now?" Chu thought for a while and replied, "Plant my tree well and live well."

This story is proof that our seven apps are never dead or dormant inside of us, no matter the age. There is purpose to every living being on this Earth. You, too, can plant your tree well and live well. The generations to come are depending on it.

Those of us who understand the responsibilities of being favor rich know that we should not have any leftovers on the inside of us when we leave Earth. You can start to pour out yourself in your latter years by recording your legacy and life lessons for future generations. This recording can be in the form of a journal, audio recordings, assessments, mentoring or story-telling, as our ancestors did.

We can easily look at characters like, Simeon, Caleb, Naomi or the widow from Zarephath as biblical examples of God's desire to use us for His purpose well into our latter years. It had been revealed to [Simeon] by the Holy Spirit that he would not see death before he had seen the Lord's Christ. (Luke 2:26). The promise was fulfilled after Simeon witnessed the presentation of

Jesus forty days after His birth. Although Simeon was senior in age, God was faithful. He is the same God today. He has a plan for seniors and wants them to be a witness and tell others that He can be trusted—God keeps His Word! Seniors are needed for their legacy, the ripened and mature skills and services they can provide is vital. Their wisdom and testimonies are invaluable life lessons. This is where genius meets senior wisdom. When the genius already on the inside of you is matured and coupled with the wisdom of your seasoned years, unimaginable feats can be accomplished.

Psalms 71:18 says, "Even when I am old and gray, do not forsake me, O God, till I declare your power to the next generation, your might to all who are to come." "They will still bear fruit in old age, they will stay fresh and green" (Psalm 92:14 NIV).

Psalm 103:1-5 reminds us that our youthfulness will be renewed when we avail ourselves for purpose at any age. The scripture reads, "…Who satisfies you with good so that your youth is renewed like the eagle's." We are reminded in Psalm 104:33 that it's never too late. "I will sing to the Lord as long as I live; I will sing praise to my God while I have being."

Don't bury the 7 apps God has given you, even in old age. Since He gave you the talent or treasure, He also will supply the provision for you to optimize the talent or treasure. Myles Munroe said the richest place on earth is the cemetery. However, I believe God is redistributing wealth that has been buried and giving it to productive, good and faithful servants of all ages. The hidden treasure in secret places like the cemetery is not hidden from God. For the Lord God is a sun and shield the Lord will give grace and glory no good thing will He withhold from them who walk uprightly. Psalms 84:11 **Although talents and treasure are different apps, the principle is still the same. Don't bury any of the 7 apps, because God put them inside of us for such a time as this to accomplish His will on earth.**

Based on the work that you have done with regard to discovering your genius, we are drawing closer to identifying your purpose. To do that, we will need to discover your hidden treasure. The key to finding your treasure lies in your ability to answer the question: **What problems are you meant to solve? Another way to state this question is what needs you are meant to fulfill? Generally, problems create needs. So, these problem/need combinations can be personal, local, and/or global.**

One important way to approach this question is to think about your past struggles. **We are often passionate about the issues that arise out of our struggles and challenges.** Sometimes we might not even be aware of how we were, and are, shaped by struggle. It might not have even been a struggle that you were conscious of. For example, a parent that is struggling with finances might be inclined to take on more than one job, basically reducing the amount of time that parent is able to spend with their child. Thus, the child who grows up feeling distant from their parent, might not realize that the genesis of that struggle was financial strain. You might spend some time thinking through these questions: 1) What struggles were your parents/guardians dealing with when you were born? 2) What early life (ages one to ten) and or young life (eleven to twenty) struggles do you recall having? 3) What struggles have you dealt with since coming into adulthood? Finally, are you passionate about any of these issues? Do you see these as potential areas in which you might add value and solve problems?

In addition to struggles, you should, on the other hand, consider your past successes and triumphs. **What needs and/or problems have you generally been successful at dealing with? We generally refer to these areas as our "knack." That is, you might have a natural knack for dealing with these types of issues. Think about times when you were successful and/ or excelled at something. What were you doing? Are you passionate about any of these issues? How did you add value and solve problems then?**

NEEDS

People have fundamental needs like food and water, and even more lofty needs, like significance. Many years ago, a psychologist by the name of Abraham Maslow suggested that we had a hierarchy of needs that ascended from physiological needs up to needs for self-actualization.

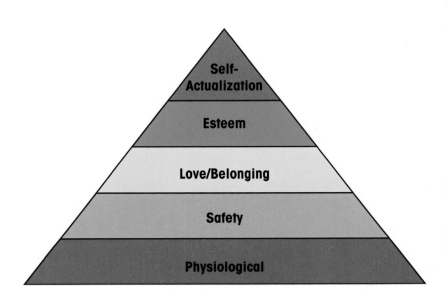

Over the years, some have challenged the validity of his theory, primarily, his suggestion that needs are hierarchically arranged. There are clearly cases where people seem to ignore their physiological and safety needs and take risks for the sake of self-actualization (e.g., bungee jumping, cliff diving...). Nevertheless, Maslow's model helped draw attention to the fact that people are motivated by fulfilling their needs. A modified model of Maslow's hierarchy is presented below:

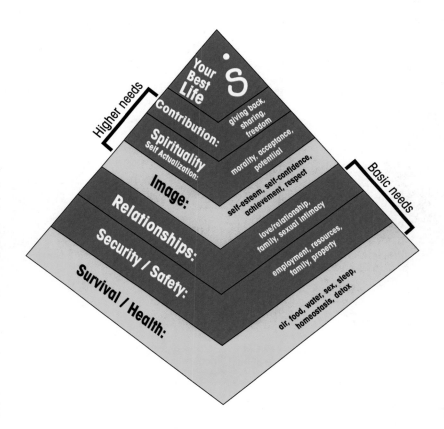

This version suggests that there are many more needs that might be even more important than those originally stated by Maslow, such as spirituality. More recently, Max-Neef developed a more elaborate classification of nine fundamental human needs:

- Subsistence
- Understanding
- Creation

- Protection
- Participation
- Identity

- Affection
- Leisure
- Freedom

In the table below, each of these needs is presented in the first column, with examples of the type of needs in the second column. In the third column are examples of what people might do to fulfill the needs listed.

Table 1–Nine Fundamental Needs

NEED	EXAMPLES	DOING - Problems I was meant to solve for others
Subsistence	physical and mental health	feed, clothe, rest, work
Protection	care, adaptability, autonomy	cooperate, plan, take care of, help
Affection	respect, sense of humor, generosity, sensuality	share, take care of, express emotions
Understanding	critical capacity, curiosity, intuition	analyze, study, meditate, investigate
Participation	receptiveness, dedication, sense of humor	cooperate, dissent, express opinions
Leisure	imagination, tranquility, spontaneity	daydream, remember, relax, have fun
Creation	imagination, boldness, inventiveness, curiosity	invent, build, design, work, compose, interpret
Identity	sense of belonging, self-esteem, consistency	get to know oneself, grow, commit oneself
Freedom	autonomy, passion, self-esteem, open-mindedness	dissent, choose, run risks, develop awareness

Thus, the lists of needs that people have are extensive and there are many ways to state needs. As mentioned earlier, needs can be stated as problems as well. **Nevertheless, based on your Genius, what needs (problems) do you think you are meant to solve for others? You may use the lists or figures above or any other list of needs you can find:**

Using my God given genius these are the problems I think I was meant to solve for others. Two problems I am meant to solve are:

_____

_____

_____

Put stars by those that appear more consistently. Each of these areas are potential "hidden treasures." That is, they are areas in which you can potentially exercise your genius.

AFFIRMATION STATEMENT

God has given me hidden treasures that are being revealed to solve problems and fulfill the needs of people that will manifest God's glory. My Treasure is the opportunities and the markets where I can solve problems and fulfill needs. I choose not to let moth and rust corrupt my treasure. I am rich toward God and man. The ideas that I implement in the earth will have eternal value and will bring dividends to me now and in the life to come. God has ordained that the treasure that I have in my earthen vessel be used in excellence for His glory and in service to my fellow man. My treasure and my heart are in alignment, which is to fully optimize the Seven Mobile Apps that God has placed within me to manifest His glory and make Him famous.

HIGHER PURPOSE

"We are more fulfilled when we are involved
in something bigger than ourselves."
– John Glenn, Astronaut

According to scientists, there are over 7 billion people on earth, technology is moving at a pace faster than we've ever seen it, and we are inundated with "connectivity" on every level. In our finite thinking, we feel smaller now and less significant, which makes us wonder if our purpose really matters in the huge scope of this universe and considering there are so many other people who seem to have a higher purpose than ours. To add to this feeling, some of us have yet to even discover what we were put on this earth to do. Like me, you may be borrowing or envious of someone else's purpose, especially if it seems more glamorous or more substantial than yours.

Here are a few facts to consider when wondering if God is concerned about your life's purpose.

Fact #1: Daily the very hairs on your head are numbered.

Fact #2: God has your name written in the palm of his hand.

Fact #3: God knows every star by name.

Scientists from the Hubble telescope estimate that there are about 200 billion stars in the Milky Way galaxy alone. I was further amazed to learn that there are also at least 100 billion additional galaxies and God is intimately aware of their purpose and uniqueness.

We are also God's workmanship, created to do good works. **When you are crystal clear and celebrate what makes you a unique individual, you will better understand your genius, what problems you were created to solve and what needs you were meant to fulfill.**

Does anyone besides me remember Alfred Matthew, known as "Weird Al" Yankovic and famous for his parody songs and videos? If just reading the name makes you chuckle, you should know that over a three-decade career he has sold more than 12 million albums, recorded more than 150 parody and original songs, and performed more than 1,000 live shows. His works have earned him four Grammy Awards and eleven nominations, four gold records, and six platinum records in the United States. This is crazy considering that although many of us know the name, most wouldn't be able to name one song title. It's even more unbelievable to think he built an entire career on being unapologetically *weird*. This is a true testament to recognizing your own uniqueness and allowing it to lead you to your higher purpose. If "Weird Al" can do this, how much more can you do?

Scientists tell us that every snowflake is different. Yet trillions of these frozen water crystals come to earth every year. These crystals have more to offer than their uniqueness and splendor. They also testify of a designer and creator whose complex solar and meteorological system has real purpose and thought. Just as the original genius and founder of this vast universe created snowflakes and made them unique, every person born also has Seven Mobile Apps that make them unique. When we are born into the earth's atmosphere, we are equipped with our own distinction and uniqueness, equipped with the potential to powerfully impact the world in a positive way through genius solutions that honor God.

We have God's DNA (Downloaded Noble Authority) inside of us to overcome everything that pertains to life that we will ever need. We have vast greatness and intense power, packed within us that goes far beyond what you can even imagine. We have access to unlimited resources that are already within us.

We are created with a higher purpose than stars in the galaxy or the snowflakes, and they indeed have a purpose. The heavens also declare God's handiwork. But because we are made in His image and likeness, and given a free will, our purpose supersedes nature in all of its splendor. No matter how successful or how unsuccessful you have been in the past, when you fully align with your inner genius and purpose and access the potential of your Seven Mobile Apps, you will optimize your life and fulfill the assignment that the Developer made specifically for you.

God is the developer of your Apps and has tailor made them for your success. He will update them if you stay connected to Him. Just like a GPS reroutes you if you take a wrong turn or get off course for any reason, so will the developer of your Apps. The rerouting is processed through your conscience.

Remember the movie, *Limitless*, starring Bradley Cooper? In the movie, he produces enhanced mental acuity. I wanted to give you that reference because it drives home the point that when you tap into your genius and purpose and the Seven Mobile Apps are optimized, they will cause you to access the limitless supply of resources available to you by the developer.

Purpose Template

Having completed all of the assessments, it's now time to put it all together and state your PURPOSE. Let's consider the following formula:

$$\textbf{GENIUS x TREASURE = PURPOSE}$$

This formula suggests that purpose is a function of one's genius and treasure. If you recall, genius refers to one's God-given and distinctive abilities, and treasure refers to the needs and/or problems that one is meant to fulfill or solve. If we put these together, then the formula suggests that our purpose is made known when we match our distinctive abilities to fundamental needs and problems that they can fulfill and solve.

The following steps walk you through putting together your purpose statement. First, let's gather all the data from the assessments. Look at your **TAGs 1, 2, 3**... What Genius areas did you list?

List your top three genius areas:

1. _____

2. _____

3. _____

Look at your **treasure** list. What problems and needs are you meant to solve and fulfill for others?

List your top three treasure areas:

1. _____

2. _____

3. _____

On the next page, fill-in the blank spaces using your lists of TAGs, and Needs list. Note: you may provide less than three.

Purpose Statement

Using my God-given Genius of (list TAGS):

_____,_____,_____,my purpose is to fulfill God's call to assist others with (list TREASURE) _____, _____, _____.

Now rewrite your purpose below without guides (parentheses and blanks) above:

_____

_____

_____

_____

_____

AFFIRMATION STATEMENT-

Everything in my life is working together for good, because I celebrate my higher purpose as a unique individual to do His purpose, and to use my God given genius to solve problems for others.

LEVERAGING FOUR STREAMS OF INCOME

"Invest in seven ventures, yes, in eight; you do not know what disaster may come upon the land."
– Ecclesiastes 11:2 (NIV)

One of the main reasons that I am an entrepreneur is because I like setting my own hours, determining my compensation and benefits package, and selecting who I want to work with. I also want the flexibility to work from home if there is inclement weather. Depending solely on a company as my single source of revenue, with the threat of layoffs, is not the type of environment that I thrive in. I have seen companies disrupt employees' lifestyles at a moment's notice by having security escort them away from their building without even collecting their personal things. Sometimes layoffs happen because the economy took a down turn and sometimes it is because their boss just does not like them that week.

A chapter in Proverbs talks about a woman who did not solely depend upon one stream of income to take care of her family. I am sure the woman entrepreneur of the year award would be given to this Proverbs 31 wife. She was utilizing her many talents, abilities, and gifts to create multiple streams of income. **Leverage is to use something that you already have**

in order to achieve something new or better. She was using what was already inside (Seven Mobile Apps) of her to make a difference in her life. She found needs and fulfilled them. She saw problems and came up with solutions. She was financially savvy.

I also read that God set Adam in the Garden of Eden which had four streams **(not just one stream)** that watered its gardens. Each of those streams had their own characteristics and their names were also significant. The four streams were named Pishon which means "increase," Gihon means "bursting forth," Tigris means "rapid," and Euphrates means "fruitfulness." God gave Adam naming rights and dominion over the earth, which included the streams. Adam used the seven apps preprogrammed within him and worked the land and subdued Eden. I believe we also have naming rights and can name our day, and the streams of income that we want to use to water our garden. In I Corinthians 6:19, God called us His garden. Here are four income streams that should be considered for your financial portfolio for the 21ˢᵗ century:

1. Services Income Stream

2. Investments Income Stream

3. Products and Passive Income Stream

4. Subject Matter Expertise Income Stream

Since I have naming rights for my income streams, I name them **SIPS**. SIPS remind me of drinking from the streams of water that are on the inside of me. As **Jesus said in scripture, "Whoever believes in me, streams of living water will flow from within him."** If you have **streams of living water within, you can allow the Seven Mobile Apps that were preprogrammed in you to stay watered and connected to the <u>Source</u> of life.** Up to **60 percent** of the human adult body is water. According to H.H. Mitchell, *Journal of Biological Chemistry 158*, the brain and heart are composed of **73 percent** water, and the lungs are about **83 percent** water. The skin contains **64 percent** water, muscles and kidneys are **79 percent water**, and even the bones are watery at 31 percent. **Because our bodies are made up of so much water, it should not be hard to imagine that streams of water are on the inside of you.**

I gave the four income streams that water my garden different names, but I believe they have the same character-istics as the four streams that watered the Garden of Eden. I want **financial** increase, that is **bursting forth**, that comes in **rapid,** and will cause **fruitfulness** to abound in my life. Thinking back on Ecclesiastes 11:2, I want to invest in seven or eight ventures so that I am financially prepared for whatever comes upon the earth. Whatever the financial climate is, I want to be ready to meet and exceed the circumstances that I face with an abundant living mindset.

Go Big & Leverage Large

You've done the hard work of discovering your talents, abilities, and gifts, as well as seeing the value in your own treasure. You have also used the Purpose formula, and now have a pretty good idea of the purpose for which you were uniquely created. Now it's time to *go big and leverage large*, which simply means to leave no stone unturned in utilizing your God-given abilities to the fullest. First and foremost, your gifts are to be used for the pre-ordained

Kingdom purpose that God intended before you were even formed in your mother's womb. At the same time, according to the Word of God, these gifts will make room (provision) for you and will put you in the presence of great men. For this to happen, we must leverage every divine relationship which are God's favor connections that will propel you to the next level for God's glory and our earthly provision.

I was child number five in a sibling group of six. Hand-me-downs from child-to-child were just a reality of my upbringing. By the age of thirteen, I wanted something different, so I began to find ways to provide for myself. I bought my own new clothes by doing various odd jobs, from cutting grass to shoveling snow. Even at that young age, I had the drive and ambition to get out there and carve a path for myself. By eighteen years old, I leveraged my organizational skills while working for an architectural firm and submitted a proposal to IBM to become their junior technician, where I proposed a solution to save the company money. Since then, I've done everything from brokering real estate to flipping homes and owning a conference center with a café and coffee-house attached. I also started a limousine service and eventually a destination management company. In each venture, I tapped into my knack for seeing the end from the beginning, and identifying market needs that God had placed in me from birth. I leveraged those talents, abilities, and gifts to fulfill the needs in my life at that time.

American psychologist Abraham Maslow's model helped to remind us that humans are motivated by fulfilling their needs.

This includes your basic natural needs as a person living in this society. In 2019, your ability to do this is largely dependent on your capacity to earn income, both active and passive. Active income is pretty straightforward, your 9 to 5, entrepreneurial ventures, and side hustles all directly contribute to your income on a consistent basis. So, let's start with the more elusive passive income. We all want it. We all want to make money without work, even while we sleep. But are there actually any good passive income ideas that we can implement this year? The answer is yes, and here are four main ways you can make income using the Investments & Products / Passive Income Streams:

- By investing money
- By investing time
- By renting things out
- By getting paid to do activities you do anyway

Understand that the most passive forms of income will require you to put up a little bit of money up-front. Warren Buffett is quoted as saying, "If you don›t find a way to make money while you sleep, you will work until you die."

Investments Income: Stream Number Two

Leverage by investing money
- Invest in dividend-paying stocks with Acorns
- Lend money in $25 increments earning 4-8%
- Put money into high-yield savings accounts

- Optimize your 401(k)
- Learn to trade the Forex Market (day trading)
- Invest in insurance products and policies
- Invest in private real estate deals with only $500 with Fundrise

Products and Passive Income: Stream Three

Leverage by investing time

- Write an e-book
- Start a drop-shipping business
- Make money off other people's YouTube videos
- Create a website to do business
- Become an Amazon Associate
- Write slogans
- Create an Online Course
- Start a blog
- Create physical products
- Create digital products

Leverage by renting things out

- Rent out your spare room
- Rent playground equipment
- Rent your stuff

Leverage by getting paid to do activities you do anyway
- Get cash back on stuff you buy anyway
- Write a song
- Create a mobile app
- Product design t-shirts
- Create a membership website and collect email addresses to sell to them
- Become an affiliate marketer without carrying inventory

Subject Matter Expertise: Income Stream Four

Subject Matter Expertise (SME) is when you are recognized as a leader in your field. The monetization of information by creating products that will help others long after you are off the scene is imperative. What have you learned about a subject matter that if people knew would solve a problem for them? What do you know that could increase the bottom line of a company or save them from making a huge mistake? What one bit of information do you know that can make someone a better negotiator if they understood a principle that you know? The SME Income Stream is often overlooked by professionals who retire or switch vocations without putting what they have learned in writing or in an electronic format for others to learn from their vast experience. SME should create products that make them money while they are sleeping. Even if you donate the money to charity or give it to a church the fact remains that a workman is worthy of his hire.

Many Subject Matter Experts work pro bono, but when they die their valuable knowledge is lost.

Services Income: Stream One

Now, let's talk about how to monetize leveraged opportunities. This is exchanging time for money. Here are a few TAG areas and ideas for turning your talents into cold, hard cash and gaining experience by developing your TAGs. The reason I included so many Service Income Streams is because it's low-hanging fruit to gain immediate cash flow using your Talents, Abilities, and Gifts so that you can see what you have a knack for doing. You should engage in the work that you answered based upon the Genius Abilities, Talent Categories and from the TAG Worksheet #1. Consider these activities and services you can provide to assist people with their endeavors, so that they can more effectively concentrate on their purpose.

Interpersonal

- Help cook for a big party
- Write thank you notes
- Write out holiday cards
- Serve food at a house party
- Help at a child's birthday or pool party
- Direct traffic in a parking lot during an event
- Guide a tour around a new town
- Assist in daily routine after an injury
- Pick up from the airport or train station
- Participate in a focus group or experiment

Spatial

- Move furniture
- Help with interior decorating
- Set up outdoor furniture after the winter

Clerical

- Return unwanted purchases
- Sync computer to devices
- Enter data into an Excel doc
- Address and mail cards
- Make reservations
- Organize and file papers
- Respond to letters and emails
- Collect mail, newspapers and packages when other people are on vacation
- Hand out flyers around town for a new business
- Scan and digitize your child's artwork

Social

- Teach basic computer skills
- Provide personal shopping
- Housesit while other people are on vacation
- Take your elderly mother grocery shopping
- Drive elderly parents to doctor's appointments
- Drive kids to soccer practice

Artistic

- Set up for a birthday party
- Create and stuff goodie bags
- Paint nails and do hair at a party for little girls

Language

- Edit college essays
- Prepare for a wedding speech or a presentation
- Edit a resume
- Rehearse a job interview

Musical/Dramatic

- Play music at an event
- Practice dances before an event

Leadership/Persuasive

- Lead a craft project at a birthday party

Numerical/Mathematical

- Stock up on essentials at a big box store

Organizational

- Organize sheds
- Do weekly grocery shopping runs
- Set up for an event (chairs, food table, drinks)
- Schedule appointments

- Assist with estate sorting after a death
- Organize CDs or records
- Organize closets
- Plan a vacation
- Clean and organize gardening and yard tools
- Organize office documents
- File and organize your recipes
- Pick up dry cleaning, alterations or clothing repairs
- Organize the garage
- Set up for a yard sale
- Organize photo albums (digital or paper)
- Clean out the attic/basement
- Organize contacts and email addresses
- Return library books -- and get new ones
- List unwanted furniture on sites like Craigslist or eBay
- Prepare guest room before family visits
- Organize a library of books
- Organize the pantry
- Organize and assist a busy professional

Manual/Technical

- Wash cars
- Rake leaves
- Clean the pool and empty the skimmers
- Haul trash to the dump
- Assemble IKEA furniture
- Put lights up for the holidays

- Shovel snow
- Mow lawns
- Weed the garden
- Paint rooms
- Water plants
- Fold laundry
- Clean the fridge
- Wash dishes
- Prep and cook meals to freeze
- Wash the windows
- Water lawns and gardens
- Bake for a bake sale
- Clean out gutters
- Clean up after a party
- Pick-up and deliver anything
- Set up electronics around the house
- Clean boat
- Dog walking
- Grill at a barbeque
- Set up a website or blog
- Wrap presents around the holidays
- Chop firewood
- Set up yard toys (trampoline, swing set, etc.)
- Pack and unpack after a move
- Deliver car for maintenance and inspections for other people

Athleticism*   Become a personal trainer

Scientific*   Become a science teacher

Become a researcher at a University

I will take SIPS from these multiple streams of income by adding them to my financial portfolio. Name at least two income streams that you have an interest in taking SIPS from.

1. Services Income Stream

---

2. Investments Income Stream

---

3. Products and Passive Income Stream

---

4. Subject Matter Expertise Income Stream

AFFIRMATION STATEMENT-

By faith and with divine direction, I go big and leverage large. I am prepared and equipped to leverage every bit of talent, ability, and genius that dwells on the inside of me. God has given me favor to attract opportunities and relationships that will advance His purpose for my life and through which He will get the glory. I will stir the world with my skills, shake the world with my talents, move the world with my brilliance, and change the world with my God-given genius. I have four streams of SIPS income that bring me financial increase, money that is bursting forth into my bank accounts, money and opportunities that comes in with rapid speed and will cause fruitfulness in my life. My fruit from my garden will remain. I am like a tree planted by the rivers of water which yields its fruit in season and my leaf does not wither— whatever I do prospers, so that I receive eternal rewards in heaven.

I leverage my finances to serve others as a cheerful, hilarious giver. God blesses me abundantly so that in all things and at all times I will have all that I need and will abound in every good work.

FAITH APP

For I say, through the grace given unto me,
to every man that is among you, not to think of himself
more highly than he ought to think; but to think soberly,
according as God hath dealt to every man
*the **measure of faith**.*
– Romans 12:3

Recently, I read an article that described ten things you did not know your phone could do. After all, with hundreds of embedded features, there are no doubt some things we have no idea about. Similarly, most people are unaware of three very important features that are included in their mobile faith app that is already inside of them. Knowledge is power. Just like the awareness needed with cell phones, you also need to study your feature manual for your mobile faith app. There's an emphasis on "mobile," because these features are transportable and can be accessed from anywhere at any time. As long as they are protected in the right case, or spiritual foundation, we are not limited by our physical location or season in life. These three features travel with us everywhere we go!

By turning on the three features below, you will become a better leader who gives good reports; you will understand the importance of knowing what pleases God; you will not be easily intimidated by others; you will become fearless; you will stand up for righteousness; regardless of your age, you will desire the promises of God; your vision will improve, and you will see yourself as an overcomer with God-sanctioned core values.

When I ask any of my three children a question about how to operate a feature in my cell phone, they say, "Let me see your phone," and then proceed to do what I need rather than show me how to do it. As a visual learner, I learn and retain best when you demonstrate for me, as opposed to just doing it for me or telling me how to do it. It has nothing to do with being from Missouri, the "Show-Me State." It has everything to do with my learning style. Once I understand a concept through insight and get a visual image (word picture) of it, I am a tenacious student who is even able to teach and communicate that same concept to others.

When the three faith app features are activated, they help us operate at a supernatural level of faith. We walk in agreement with God to see, behave and react in faith. When we consistently walk in faith, we inspire others to look beyond their natural realm to solve problems they otherwise thought impossible. Another feature causes us to live by a higher code of conduct. We don't react in fear when perilous situations arise. Rather, we respond in faith.

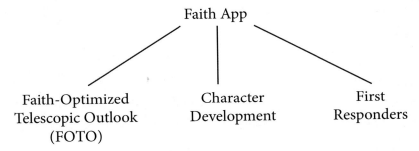

Faith App

Faith-Optimized Telescopic Outlook (FOTO)   Character Development   First Responders

Feature #1: Faith Optimized Telescopic Outlook (FOTO)

I may be showing my age again, but do you remember the television series popular in the 1970s, *The Six Million Dollar Man*? I loved it. The main character, played by actor Lee Majors, had bionic implants that gave him superhuman strength and power, including a bionic eye that let him see through objects and at distances that others could not. *The Bionic Woman* came later as a spinoff series. Just imagine being able to see things otherwise hidden to the naked eye and this being given to you as a superpower. Well, Well, I'm here to share the good news, when activated you have a bionic feature inside of you. You can have superhero insight and vision according to your "measure of faith."

The faith app on the inside of you has an optimization characteristic that allows you to use the <u>F</u>aith <u>O</u>ptimized <u>T</u>elescopic <u>O</u>utlook (FOTO) feature to visualize the end of a matter at the beginning, regardless of what the natural eye can see. FOTO is your bionic eye. The Telescopic Outlook feature allows you to optimize your vision and see things that are far away, as if they were up close. Focusing on the desired outcome is a life principle that everyone should apply, because it will give you optimism throughout the process of whatever endeavor you undertake.

Once you activate the FOTO feature, it will give you the confidence to produce a personal visual image that reminds you of want you desire to happen, whether it is a goal, a possession, a place, an accomplishment, a destiny, impact on others, etc.

My Real Estate

When I was renovating real estate, I would hire an architect to draw a 3D rendering of the anticipated finished product. I would envision what the property would look like upon completion. Regardless of the horrific present condition of the property or the setbacks and obstacles I encountered during the renovation process, I was able to endure whatever hardships came my way because I was focused on the outcome. The process of renovating the property built character and stick-to-itiveness in me to meet deadlines and honor commitments, which were invaluable in building a business of integrity with a solid reputation.

Jesus' Empty Tomb/Empty Rugged Cross

Similarly, Jesus, as the author and finisher of our faith, did not enjoy the cross, but He endured it, despising the shame because of the joy that was set before Him. It is imperative that you keep your eyes on the prize when facing challenging times or even persecution. Even though you may suffer, you will learn things along the way, just as Jesus learned obedience through the things He suffered. We also should be obedient as we are going through the process of struggle and development. As a matter of fact, the **empty** old rugged cross is a visual image that Christians should use as the FOTO to remind us of our eternal and earthly goals.

Our purpose on earth gains tremendous encouragement considering the fact that we have a risen Savior who has the authority and power to help us in our life endeavors. The grave could not hold him. He took the sting out of death and the forces of the dark side could not keep him in the borrowed tomb. Jesus is the epitome of using his FOTO and was able to visualize God raising him from the dead.

As a case in point, Jesus said, "as Jonah was in the belly of the whale for three days and three nights, so shall the son of man be in the heart of the earth for three days and three nights." The visual image that Jesus used was Jonah in the belly of the whale.

What are you using to remind yourself of the promises of God in your life? What visual images are you using to see your children serving God, or your business making a major impact and solving problems for others? What goals do you have that seem impossible? Activate the faith app that is already inside of you, because it will improve your vision and give you hope and a strategy to hold on to.

A Father Saw His Prodigal Son from Afar

A son wanted his inheritance, so his father divided his property between his two sons. The son went to a far-off country and wasted his inheritance money. After becoming broke, he went to work for someone else in a pig's pen. But he remembered his father's servants ate better than he was eating, so he went back home to ask for forgiveness. The expectation of his father is the point in this story. Although the prodigal son was far off, it did not stop the father from looking. I imagine he went many days to the road looking for his son, but the son was not there yet. "…but while he was still a long way off, his father saw him and was filled with compassion for him; he ran to his son, threw his arms around him and kissed him." Luke 5:20 I imagine that his father used his FOTO to see his son far away (telescopic outlook). What visual image can you use to see your child come back home in obedience to God and serving him? Is it a picture of him/her taken years ago when they were attending church regularly? What do you have the confidence to produce as a reminder of the petition you have before God?

Elijah Could See Rain Even Though it had not Rained in Years

Another biblical story that expresses the dependability of the promises of God is about the prophet Elijah and the promise of rain. He also used his FOTO to see the faraway promise. Elijah believed God would send rain and said to his servant said "Go up now, and look toward the sea." So, the servant went up and looked and said, "There is nothing." And Elijah retorted, "Go back" seven times. It came about at the *seventh time* that he said, "Behold, a cloud as small as a man's hand is coming up from the sea." And Elijah said, "Go up, say to Ahab, 'Prepare *your chariot* and go down, so that the *heavy* shower does not stop you.'" In a little while, the sky grew black with clouds and wind, and there was a heavy shower. Just like Elijah, even before the manifestation of rain appears, we also must look through the eyes of faith for our promise. It might be years before the natural manifestation, but if we can have a telescopic outlook, even though we might only see a visual image that is small in size, no bigger than the palm of your hand, just know that the promise is coming, and it will pour down in your life like a flood. Your FOTO is creating a photo image or visual image of what you believe you have received from God by faith in the spiritual realm that has not yet been manifested in the natural realm.

Abraham Could See Thousands of Years in the Future

Abraham used his FOTO, as he believed God for his descendants to multiply and become a nation. God gave Abraham a visual image to remind him of his promise, "I will surely bless you and make your descendants as numerous as the **stars in the sky** and as the **sand on the seashore**." Anytime Abraham wanted to be encouraged about the future of his descendants, he could look up and see the **stars or look down and see the sand on the shore**. When God made this promise to Abraham, He only had

Isaac and Ishmael. But look at his seed today. In fact, Jesus said Abraham used his telescopic view to look down through history thousands of years before Jesus was born and saw Jesus' day and rejoiced! Don't be shortsighted. With your FOTO, you can see far into the future.

Job Could See Beyond the Grave

Job was a very wealthy man in the Bible, and seemingly lost everything he had. His ten children were all killed in the same day; he lost his cattle and livestock; and his body was wracked with boils and sores. His wife tells him to "curse God and die." Throughout that entire situation, Job was convinced about his purpose. He said," "All the days of my appointed time will I wait, till my change come." He further emphasized, "You shall call, and I will answer You, You shall desire the work of Your hands." Job understood that God holds us accountable for the works we do in this life. Even though he knows he is destined for the grave and that his body will turn into worms, he could see beyond the grave using his FOTO!

Can you see beyond the grave? The purpose for which God made you is going to be accounted for, so are you ready to start living and seeing beyond this life? Job was convinced that he could see the future with his faith being optimized while looking through his telescopic lens. He asked the question, "If a man dies will he live again?" He answered his own question and said, "I know my redeemer liveth, and that he shall stand at the latter day upon the earth:

And though after my skin worms destroy this body, yet in my flesh shall I see God: Whom I shall see for myself, and mine eyes shall behold, and not another; though my reins be consumed within me" Job 19:23-27.

Feature Number Two: Character Development Faith

Your faith app will impact your character development. Warren Buffett is quoted as saying that intelligence, integrity, and energy are the three most important things he would like for every employee to have. The question then becomes, can your character keep you where your talents, abilities, and gifts (TAG) make room for you?

From Jim Bakker to Bill Cosby, O.J. Simpson and Harvey Weinstein, there are countless instances where a beloved and respected celebrity falls hard from grace because of a lack of character or issues with integrity. Who today hasn't heard of the socially viral #MeToo movement? There's one man and eighty reports behind it all. At age sixty-six, Harvey Weinstein has spent a career co-founding and building a highly successful enter-tainment and production company, the Weinstein Company. In October 2017, more than eighty women accused him of sexual assault, which included accusations of rape. Weinstein allegedly abused his position of power to coerce and assault many actresses. Consequently, he was kicked off the board of his *own company* and was banned from the Producers Guild for life. Criminal charges were also being pursued against him. There's no better example of having it all and losing it, because of a lack of integrity and character.

Character development is living life in honor of the sacrifice that Jesus Christ made on Calvary's Cross! It's presenting our bodies as a living sacrifice holy acceptable unto the Lord which is our reasonable service, which means to live by God's code of ethics. This standard places a demand on us to conduct business and our personal affairs in a manner that when people see your good works, it brings honor and glory to God. It's time to have character that matches your faith. Based on who you say you serve, it's high time to show your faith by your works.

Tyler Perry is an award-winning entertainment mogul with nineteen movies, twenty stage plays, seven running television shows and two bestselling books under his belt. In a 2013 segment of *CBS This Morning's* "Note to Self'" special, Tyler was asked to write a letter to his thirteen-year-old self. He wrote, "As I search your young face for any sign of myself, believe it or not, I'm able to smile, because just behind all of that darkness, I see hope. You've got some kind of faith in God, little boy. I know you don't know this right now, but who you will become is being shaped inside every one of those experiences, every one of them, the good, the bad, and yes, even the really ugly ones."

Those who know Tyler's testimony know that he was physically and sexually abused as a young boy and later ended up homeless in pursuit of his dreams. Through his many accomplishments, he has shown us what is possible when your faith matches your work and you allow God to develop your character through trials. He recognized in this letter that he even had great faith as a little boy in the midst of some horrific circumstances.

In this political climate, it seems harder to recognize people whose faith and actions line up with the Word of God. But there are people who still believe that a good name is to be chosen above riches, wealth, and even fame. Our character ought to line up with the earthly example of Jesus, especially since we are told to model His behavior. A WWJD (What Would Jesus Do) bracelet could serve as a reminder on how to act in certain situations and that our faith and actions should match, and not just be lip service. But rather we should want to honor God in our actions, because we might be the only Bible someone will ever read. Your faith has to be developed under fire. In business relationships, your character will be tested in the areas of honesty, integrity, truthfulness, punctuality, effectiveness, etc.

Secondly, character development is living by core values, principles, and morals according to the Bible. The Ten Commandments do not have an updated version, because our society norms have changed. God has not changed his mind about sin. It is a reproach to any people or nation. How you do things matter and why you do things matter even more. Don't be fooled, God is not going to be mocked, what a man sows, that he shall reap. Choose life by doing right things for the right reasons. Help people who are hurting, and you will touch God's heart. If you solve problems for others with your genius, activate your faith in living out God's purpose for your life, and optimize the other apps within you, nothing shall be impossible to you.

Thirdly, having put my faith in Jesus Christ and developing an attitude of being totally dependent upon his grace, I have determined that if I fall down seven times, I will get up eight times. I will keep my confidence in him that is able to keep me from falling and to present me faultless before God, because of his sacrifice for me.

Character development is not just a set of rules and regulations to follow, so that our works will get us in heaven. Works can't get us there. Rather it is our commitment and conscious effort to show our gratitude for the sacrifice of the finished work that Jesus did on Calvary's cross. Our works alone aren't sufficient to gain relationship with God. It is only when we add faith (in Jesus Christ's work on the cross) to our works that we become people who have eternal hope through our faith.

Can you visualize how you can use your talents, abilities, and gifts for the good of others? Visualize how you can use uncovered treasure to positively affect the market or opportunity that you were meant to fulfill. You are well able, with overwhelming faith, to do the impossible. Without faith, it is impossible to please God. But with faith, no mountain, struggle or obstacle can stop you from achieving your purpose.

First Responders

On September 11, 2001, as I was watching television when the attack in New York City happened, I saw brave men and women put themselves in harm's way to save people they did not even know.

I saw when one of the twin towers fell and killed many people, including the first responders on the ground. I started screaming at the television, begging the additional first responders not to go into the second tower, because it would probably be attacked also. The first responders went into the second tower anyway, despite the clear and present danger. Because of the training these selfless first responders had received, they headed toward adversity in a chaotic emergency situation, when others were running away from it.

Twelve Spies Check Out the Promised Land

Here is a story of twelve other first responders that put themselves in harm's way despite facing giants as their opponents. And the Lord spoke to Moses, saying, "Send men to spy out the land of Canaan, which I am giving to the children of Israel; from each tribe of their fathers you shall send a man, everyone a leader among them." (Numbers 13:2) Twelve spies went out to see if the land was as God promised, and ten came back with an evil report, saying, "there are giants in that land and we look like grasshoppers in our sight and their sight also." Only Caleb and Joshua came back with a good report. First Responders Faith agrees with God quickly, and those who possess it have an extraordinary spirit within them. Joshua and Caleb were ready to go toward the adversity, not run away because they were afraid of the monumental task.

David and Goliath

David ran toward Goliath while his brothers and Israel's army were hiding. David's opponent was an uncircumcised, intimidating, nine-feet-six-inches tall Philistine giant. He was hurling insults at David, the people of Israel, and their God. Despite being dismissed as the smaller, younger brother, David repeatedly asked for the opportunity to fight and defend. This means he willingly signed up to run toward the adversity. In fact, he was originally only on fighting turf to deliver food and water to his older brothers. When he heard the giant's taunts and insults, where his brothers, like the other men there were paralyzed with fear and intimidated by the size of the giant, David trusted his faith apps and only saw an opportunity to fulfill his purpose and conquer. All those years herding sheep developed David's character and prepared him in heart, mind, and spirit to be a first responder in the challenge that would define his destiny.

Take Your Genius Toward Life's Adversity

Like David, be a first responder in your own life. Use your genius to run toward the adversity of life. Trust God and follow your genius insight through prayer to solve any problem. God has equipped you to overcome and dominate in this life. You are His workmanship, created in Christ Jesus to do good works. He is inside of you to help you in every way. First Responders Faith is like Joshua and Caleb's mindset, when they said, " Let us go up at once", they wanted to do what God said immediately. That's my attitude!

Being a First Responder is using your genius to solve a problem that you were created to solve. The idea is to run toward adversity. When God gives you an assignment, your first response to the challenge or adversity should be that I am more than able to accomplish the task before me.

FOTO means having enough confidence to produce a visual image of what you have already received from God by faith. Don't just use it for personal gain and material stuff. Instead, use your difference-making spiritual attitude to enhance the Kingdom of God, which will fulfill your Purpose App. Use your affirmations to express how you see yourself and what you believe the image of God is for you.

FOTO, character development, and a First Responders mindset is *Now faith*. When you combine FOTO, character development, and First Responders faith together, they are enough to make you stand out from the crowd. You will have a different spirit, mindset, and attitude than the rest of the leaders! Understand that you have creative words in your mouth that can influence people for the good or bad, so choose to encourage people to be great and to do good.

A First Responder is ready to act at once with an attitude of, *"If God said it, let's do it. If God said it, then I know the provision will accompany the promise."* It's imperative that you use your eyes of faith and see through the telescopic lens of the spirit to envision whatever you are striving for as an accomplished reality. Faith, with your daily affirmations will help you have what you See and Say.

Jesus was and is the Visual Aid to Show us What God is Like

Jesus said, "If you have seen me you have seen the Father." God also expressed the importance of a visual aid by providing us an example of Him. Hebrews 1:3 says, "Who being the brightness of his glory, and the express image of his person…". Humankind needed to know what God was like, since no one had ever seen God, but we wanted to know Him and have a relationship with God. So, God so loved the world that He gave his only begotten son that whosoever believed in him should not die but have everlasting life. If you want to know what God is like and you need a visual aid, look no further than His Son, Jesus the Christ, the Savior of the world.

AFFIRMATION STATEMENT

My mobile faith app has an optimization feature which allows me to visualize the end of a matter from the beginning and see things that are far off in the future as if they were up close.

I received the attribute from God that gives me the authority to declare life and victorious living in this present life and the one to come.

God sees the end from the beginning, and because He sees the past, future, and present all at the same time, He has good plans for me to prosper and to bring me to that expected end.

The end of a matter is better than its beginning. But I will not despise small beginnings, because through the process of time, God is doing a great work in me.

I have great character and integrity as displayed by my faith. I live by principles, core values, and honesty that are based upon the Word of God and that will outlast the test of time.

I will focus on the end result and endure tough circumstances, tribulation, patience, and obedience through things I learn. I have the confidence to produce personal visual images that remind me of the goals I want to achieve. I visualize maximizing my talents, abilities, and gifts.

With God I am well able to accomplish the impossible. I call those things which be not as though they were. I belong to Christ and I am Abraham's seed, which means I am an heir according to the promises of God.

I visualize living my life in honor of the sacrifice made for me on Calvary's Cross.

I am a First Responder. I have a different spirit in me that says, "Let's us go up at once and take the land of promise." I am a leader that brings a good report that is in agreement with God's Word.

I see myself as more than a conqueror.

FAVOR APP

"And unto one he gave five talents, to another two, and to another one; to every man according to his own ability...."
– Matthew 25:15

There is a popular term about the favor of God that we all love to quote, *"Favor ain't fair!"* It feels good rolling off the tongue, because we all relish in the thought of unmerited preference and entitlement. Although I agree that favor may not always feel fair to onlookers, let me step out on a limb and say that favor isn't free either. Yes, it's unmerited, and yes, it is freely given by grace. However, this is not the same as being free of expectation or requirement. According to the Word of God, *to whom much is given, much is required.* My three children, as I'm sure with yours, are freely given anything I have. It's my pleasure to show grace and favor to each one of them according to God's provision for our family, but there is an expectation of responsibility, thankfulness, and giving back to bless others as they have been blessed. The same is true of God's favor in our lives. Favor in your life is manifestation of our Heavenly Father's approval and validation of us as His offspring, and it can only be received and used for His purpose if you are an open recipient.

F – Father's
A – Approval
V – Validating
O – Open
R – Recipients

The fact that we have the Father's approval is validated by the mere fact that we are benefiting as open recipients of His grace evidenced by the very air that we breathe. Our Favor App is freely given by His grace, but just as we've grown accustomed to looking for the apps on our phone with the word FREE beside them, we know that there are still terms of usage and a process for agreeing to accept those terms before having access. There are Three **Favor App Features that come with responsibilities that we must accept the terms of: Stewardship, Intentional Acts of Kindness, and God's Glory**.

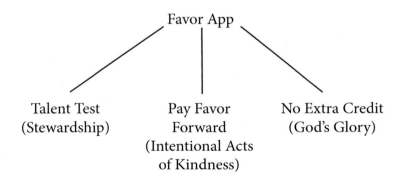

App Feature Number One: TALENT TEST (Stewardship)

Many are familiar with the Parable of the Talents in Chapter 25 of the Book of Matthew, where a man who was about to take a journey entrusted all his possessions in the care of his servants. It reads, "To one he gave five talents, to another, two, and to another, one, each according to his own ability; and then he went on his journey." The parable never indicates that he expressed his expectation to the servants or gave any detailed instruction about what to do with it.

After a long journey, the master returned. The parable goes on to say, "The one who had received the five talents went at once and traded with them, and he [made a profit and] gained five more. Likewise, the one who had two [made a profit and] gained two more. But the one who had received the one went and dug a hole in the ground and hid his master's money."

When the master learned of what each had done with what he had been given, his response to the two servants who had doubled their talents was, "Well done, good and faithful servant. You have been faithful and trustworthy over a little, I will put you in charge of many things; share in the joy of your master." To the one who had buried his one talent in a hole in the ground, he said, "You wicked, lazy servant…" Furious that the servant hadn't at least put it in a bank to accrue interest, he then took that servant's one talent and gave it to the one with ten.

If a mere man would expect stewardship from his servants, how much more do you think God expects of us, his beloved children? Just as this master told his servants, if we are faithful over a little, God will make us ruler over much. Think about the times over the course of your life when God has supernaturally supplied needs; opened doors that should have been closed; brought divine connections in your life that could have been missed if you'd left the house just seconds later; protected you in environments where others were hurt or killed; and gave you ideas that you know beyond the shadow of doubt came straight from the throne. These all demonstrate God's favor, and all these scenarios come with an expectation of stewardship.

Don't be like the servant with one talent who was afraid and made excuses for his poor stewardship by declaring, "So I was afraid [to lose the talent], and I went and hid your talent in the ground." Fear will make you overly cautious, which leads to inaction. God is a God of action, and therefore, is never pleased when we allow fear to paralyze our progress. The master not only called this servant lazy, but also called him wicked. If God did not give us a Spirit of fear, but of love, power, and a sound (disciplined) mind, then we have to assume fear is the opposite of these things. And if God is love, then fear is wicked, and it leads to a lack of power and discipline.

We are also reminded of the responsibility of stewardship when we consider another popular parable, The Parable of Ten Virgins which is found in Matthew 25. In this story, the Kingdom of Heaven is compared to ten virgins who took their lamps to meet the bridegroom. The scripture reads, "Five of them were foolish [thoughtless, silly, and careless], and five were wise [far-sighted, practical, and sensible].[3] For when the foolish took their lamps, they did not take any [extra] oil with them, but the wise took flasks of oil along with their lamps." As the parable goes, the bridegroom was delayed and took longer than expected to arrive, but the wise virgins were prepared and still able to have light in their lamps to go out and meet him. The foolish virgins were not. They attempted and failed to convince the wise virgins to share their oil and were left having to go and buy more. These foolish virgins tried to hurry and catch up in time for the wedding feast, but they were too late and were not permitted to enter. In fact, when they knocked on the door, the response was, "…I assure you and most solemnly say to you, I do not know you [we have no relationship]." The parable ends with the admonishment, "Therefore, be on the alert [be prepared and ready], for you do not know the day nor the hour [when the Son of Man will come].

None of us know the time or the hour when God's favor will be granted, but as good stewards, we must always be prepared, courageous, and disciplined. With your "free" Favor App, there are features, which still come with terms of use. Stewardship is included in those terms. Remember that stewardship is required every time you pull up your Favor App and see the word FREE next to it.

App Feature #2: PAY FAVOR FORWARD (Intentional Acts of Kindness)

If those who haven't proclaimed salvation publicly understand the principal of giving back, then how much more should believers who are saved by the blood of Jesus Christ understand our responsibility to pay favor forward through intentional acts of charity and kindness?

Warren Buffett is well-known and famously quoted for his philosophy of giving back. In fact, some would arguably say he's more famous for his charitable donations than his billionaire status. People have come to admire him as much for his philosophies on charitable giving as his success in the financial arena as chairman and CEO of Berkshire Hathaway. These philanthropic acts include a recent donation of $3.17 billion to the Bill and Melinda Gates Foundation and giving away more than $46 billion since 2000. The eighty-five-year-old has been quoted as saying he expects to have given away ninety-nine percent of his portfolio when he leaves this earth. Of course, his billionaire bud, Bill Gates, isn't far behind him in the race to pay it forward. I know, these are big numbers. You might be thinking, "Well, I don't have billions to give away or, even thousands. This is easy for billionaires to do, but not me." This just isn't true. It's easy for any of us, according to our commitment to stewardship. According to Giving USA, *regular* people, everyday working Joes, were the biggest source of charitable donations in 2012, donating an estimated $228.9 billion. Likewise, it's well-documented that Barrack Obama won the presidency off five and ten-dollar donations from millions who supported him, rather than millions of dollars from a few wealthy donors.

The parable of the talents teaches us that it's all relative. Remember, one was given ten, one five, and the other one. The same is true for what each of us may have been given with which to be charitable, and we all know that being intentionally kind costs us nothing. So, it doesn't matter what amount you have in the bank. What percentage of that amount are you intentionally giving back in various ways charitable donations, blessing someone with a place to stay in the home God has favored you to get, giving a ride to someone even when inconvenient in the car you've been blessed with, paying for someone's coffee at Starbucks, sowing your time and offerings in a ministry that spiritually feeds you.

We also learn from a widow woman in 1 Kings 17 that God will bless your sacrifice of a little no differently than the billions given by the wealthy. If you recall, in this scripture, Elijah had prophesied that a drought was coming. He was on a journey with God's assurance of provision when the brook dried up leaving him thirsty. A word of the Lord commanded him to go to a certain land where he'd find a widow woman who would provide for him. When Elijah arrived, the widow told him, "As the LORD your God lives, I have no bread, only a handful of flour in the bowl and a little oil in the jar. See, I am gathering a few sticks so that I may go in and bake it for me and my son, that we may eat it [as our last meal] and die."

Elijah assured her that if she used the little she had to supply his need, that God had given him a word saying, "The bowl of flour shall not be exhausted nor shall the jar of oil be empty until the day that the LORD sends rain [again] on the face of the earth." The widow did as Elijah had instructed and not only was there an endless supply of flour and oil for her house but her son was also raised from the dead.

Being intentional means just that. It means waking up with the very intent to be a vessel used to be a blessing to someone whether through a gift, smile, or act of service. What a blessing for this woman to be called out by God to be a blessing to one of His chosen prophets. Since we have received favor from God, let us TAG others with random and intentional acts of kindness. Let's pay favor forward to everyone in our sphere, to any and all that we can touch with our genius.

App Feature Number Three: NO EXTRA CREDIT (God's Glory)

There is a quote by an unknown author that says, "If your success is neither attributable to you nor luck, then perhaps you have the favor of God upon you." It ends with the well-known proverb, "Give credit where credit is due."

Remember being able to get extra credit when you were in school, and surely most of us also remember end-of-year awards ceremonies? It's been engrained in us since we were very young to both expect unmerited extra credit to help make up for our deficiencies or lack of preparation earlier in the semester, but then we look forward to proudly displaying what we consider our earned awards at the close of the school year. Is it fair that a student who made up for earlier slack with extra credit gets to earn an award ahead of another student who maybe worked twice as hard all yearlong with only average results? Maybe not, but it teaches the lesson very early that favor ain't fair.

The difference when we become adults and fully mature in our spiritual walk is that we understand that we cannot take a walk across that figurative stage and smugly accept the medal at the end of this race. We can't smirk at our classmate who struggled to get a C and think how superior we are. And we can't pat ourselves on the back for taking full advantage of the extra credit we've been given. In this race, we give God the glory in all things. In this acceptance speech, we first give honor to God for freely giving us something that we could never earn, His favor.

In 1 Corinthians 6:20, we are reminded that we are not our own, but rather, "You were bought with a price [you were actually purchased with the precious blood of Jesus and made His own]." If we keep in mind that we don't even belong to ourselves, it will be that much easier to protect ourselves against a spirit of pride as God's favor propels us upward, 'lest we become like Satan himself, who was so puffed up with pride that he began exalting himself above God. And we know how that story ends.

Our Favor App is there for our benefit, but first and foremost, for God's fulfillment of His purpose on this Earth through us. In all the favor you will ever be granted in this life, God gets all the glory, so that his glory may be manifested in your life. There is nothing given to you that doesn't come from our Father in Heaven and credit should be given to our Lord as such. This time, there is no extra credit for you, but guess what? You still get to reap the rewards at the end of the race.

Being *Favor Rich* is about being God's Intelligent Tool (His genius) in the earth to solve problems for others by applying God's wisdom. Favor is a benefit that everyone has as God's offspring and as open recipients of His grace, whether you recognize it as His favor or not.

The technological scientific original design in humans far exceeds the artificial intelligence in robots that man has been able to produce millions of years later. The Seven Mobile Apps within us, and our brain that functions as a supercomputer, are more intelligent than any other creation of God's. These truths alone testify of a God who spared no expense in the creation of His design and most prized possession. If you are a believer, you are filled with favor, because you are a son or daughter of the Most High. Now activate those features and show the world what increasing favor looks like!

In 2nd Corinthians 8:9 we read "For you know the grace (unmerited favor) of our Lord Jesus Christ, that though he was rich, yet for your sake he became poor, so that you through his poverty might become rich." **We all received the blessing of becoming favor rich at birth and we became an offspring of the creator of the universe. But there are different levels of favor that you can receive in life to experience an exponential increase in favor with God and man.**

Here are three things you can do to increase the favor in your life:

- **Become a Born Again Believer** by accepting Jesus Christ as your personal Savior. Romans 10:9-11 says, "That if thou shalt confess with thy mouth the

Lord Jesus, and shalt believe in thine heart that God hath raised him from the dead, thou shalt be saved. For with the heart man believeth unto righteousness; and with the mouth confession is made unto salvation… whosoever believeth on him shall not be ashamed."

- **Become a Better Steward** of his Word and by optimizing all Seven Mobile Apps that are inside of you. Find your inner genius and solve the problem(s) that you were created to solve. Leverage what God has already given you and become a subject matter expert in what you're passionate about. Remember the principle from the parable of the talents— "use it or lose it."

- **Become a Daily Affirmation Guru** by saying what God says about you for five minutes every day. Isaiah 65:16 says, "Because he who blesses himself on the earth will bless himself by the God of truth *and* faithfulness. Remember that death and life is in the power of the tongue. Christians bless the Lord regularly at church, we even bless people who curse us and try to do us harm and rightfully so. But we need to take the time to replenish and bless ourselves with daily confessions that affirm that we have the *F*ather's *A*pproval and He has *V*alidated us as *O*pen *R*ecipients. (FAVOR)

AFFIRMATION STATEMENT

God has favored me as his most prized creation. Within me is a Favor App that attracts divine opportunity, ideas, and relationships into my life. When I am favored to receive these things, I am a good steward who is well-prepared and disciplined. I give back, as I am freely given, through charitable donations and intentional acts of kindness. I give God all the glory, honor, and praise for the favor that shows up in my life, whether I recognize it as such or not. I am a favor magnet and my life demonstrates it in every area.

FAVOR RICH PRODUCTS & SERVICES

For a deeper dive into the Favor Rich principles and tools, here are a few Favor Rich products and services available to take your efforts to discover your purpose and leverage your genius to the next level.

PRODUCTS & RESOURCES

(all listed products, services & resources can be found on the Favor Rich website at www.FavorRich.com, by clicking the 'Products' or 'Services' tab)

Favor Rich E-Book
Loved your hard copy of *Favor Rich* and want to purchase or gift the electronic version? Visit the Favor Rich website to purchase the e-book.

Favor Rich Audio Book
Take Favor Rich everywhere you go with the audio book version narrated by Coach Cal himself. To download, visit the Favor Rich website.

Favor Rich Online Course
Become a student of the many ways in which you can leverage your inner genius through a Favor Rich online course. Visit the website for details and to register.

Favor Rich Journal & E-Journal
Enhance your journey with a journal or e-journal custom designed for *Favor Rich* students. Both can be found on the Favor Rich website.

Become a Member of the Favor Rich Online Community

Get to know like-minded individuals by becoming a member of the Favor Rich online community at www.FavorRich.com. Membership will give you access to even more tools, tips and information to propel you forward. Join today!

COACHING & TRAINING SERVICES

Personal & Business Coaching

Discover your genius with Coach Cal as your guide. He will tailor a coaching or training package that's just right for you or your business. Schedule some time to develop a custom plan to best leverage your talents, abilities and gifts.

Online & Virtual Coaching

The part of the region in which you live shouldn't hinder your access to life-changing coaching and fulfillment of your genius. Register for a **Favor Rich** online or virtual coaching session.

Keynote Speaker

As a business owner and an ordained minister, you can count on Coach Cal to motivate and educate your business or civic group with wisdom and wit. Book Coach Cal as your next event's dynamic keynote speaker.